Date: 3/22/16

J 599.638 BEL
Bell, Samantha,
Meet a baby giraffe /

LIGHTNING
BOLT
BOOKS

Meet a Baby Giraffe

Samantha S. Bell

Lerner Publications
Minneapolis

Content Consultant: Dr. Mark C. Andersen, Department of Fish Wildlife and Conservation Ecology, New Mexico State University

Lerner Publications Company
A division of Lerner Publishing Group, Inc.
241 First Avenue North
Minneapolis, MN 55401 USA

For reading levels and more information, look up this title at www.lernerbooks.com.

Library of Congress Cataloging-in-Publication Data

Bell, Samantha.
    Meet a baby giraffe / Samantha S. Bell.
        pages   cm — (Lightning Bolt Books™—Baby African animals)
        ISBN 978-1-4677-7975-3 (lb : alk. paper) — ISBN 978-1-4677-8361-3 (pb : alk. paper) —
ISBN 978-1-4677-8362-0 (EB pdf)
        1. Giraffe—Infancy—Juvenile literature. I. Title.
    QL737.U56B45 2014
    599.63813'92—dc23   2014038833

Manufactured in the United States of America
1 – BP – 7/15/15

Table of Contents

A Tall Baby — page 4

Safe with Mom — page 10

Let's Eat! — page 16

Out on the Grasslands — page 22

Habitat in Focus — page 28

Fun Facts — page 29

Glossary — page 30

Further Reading — page 31

Index — page 32

A Tall Baby

After fifteen months, it is finally time! A mother giraffe is ready to have her baby. A baby giraffe is called a calf. Giraffes usually have one calf at a time. Sometimes they have twins.

This mother giraffe cleans her newborn calf.

A newborn calf is about 6 feet (2 meters) tall and weighs 220 pounds (100 kilograms). That's about the size of a grown man!

A baby giraffe looks a lot like its parents. It has a spotted coat, two short horns, and a stiff mane.

A calf's mother and father are 14 to 18 feet (4 to 5.5 m) tall. They weigh between 1,750 and 2,800 pounds (790 and 1,270 kg), almost as much as a small car.

Adult giraffes are so tall they could reach the top of a one-story house.

A mother giraffe helps her newborn take its first steps.

A new calf can stand up when it is one hour old. After just ten hours, it can run with its mother!

A mother giraffe takes care of her baby by herself for the first few weeks. Then they both join the herd.

Baby giraffes stay close to their mothers.

There are five to forty giraffes in a herd. They are males and females of all ages.

Safe with Mom

In the herd, baby giraffes are part of a nursery group. They explore and play together.

One mother watches over the calves while the other giraffes look for food.

It is hard for lions, hyenas, and leopards to see calves in the grass.

The calves' spotted coats blend in with the grass. This helps keep them hidden.

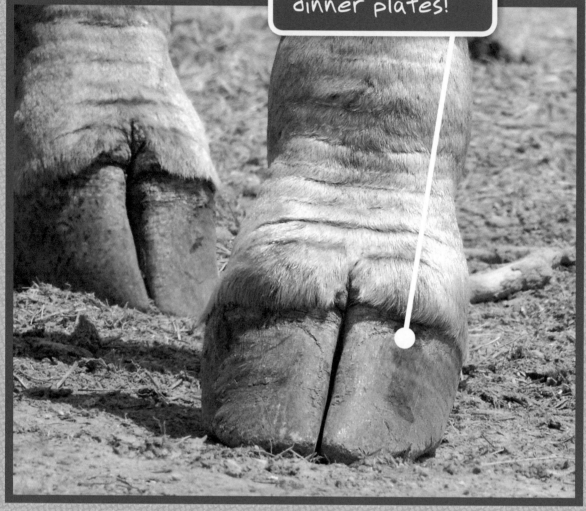

Giraffe hooves are as big as dinner plates!

A mother giraffe protects her baby. She kicks predators with her big hooves. Each hoof is 12 inches (31 centimeters) across!

Giraffes seem quiet. But they make many different sounds. They grunt or snort to warn other giraffes of danger.

Giraffes also moan, snore, and hiss.

Mother giraffes sometimes whistle to their calves. Calves answer them by bleating.

Mothers whistle for their calves when they get too far away.

14

This growing calf is almost as tall as its mother.

A calf grows about 4 feet (1 m) in the first year. Now it is 10 feet (3 m) tall. That is as tall as a basketball goal.

Let's Eat!

A newborn calf is hungry. It starts nursing as soon as it can stand. It will drink its mother's milk for nine to twelve months. At about four months, it starts eating leaves from trees and shrubs.

A giraffe can reach leaves that are high up in trees with its long tongue.

The calf and its mother use their long tongues to pull leaves from the branches. An adult giraffe's tongue is 1.5 to 2 feet (0.5 to 0.6 m) long. That is about as long as your arm.

A mother giraffe and her calf eat together.

The mother and baby chew the leaves and swallow them. Then the food comes back up.

The giraffes chew their food again. This is called chewing their cud.

Sometimes giraffes chew their cud for hours.

Giraffes get water from the leaves they eat.

Giraffes get thirsty too. But they do not need to drink every day.

Sometimes giraffes drink at a water hole. This puts them in danger. They must spread their legs far apart to reach the water. Giraffes can't quickly run away when they stand like this.

Giraffes can't make a fast escape if a predator comes to a watering hole.

Out on the Grasslands

A giraffe leaves its mother to find a mate.

A calf leaves its mother when it is fifteen to eighteen months old. A giraffe is fully grown between three and five years old. Now females can give birth to their own calves.

Giraffes spend most of their time eating. They munch on leaves, flowers, fruit, and vines from the treetops.

Giraffes sleep for only about thirty minutes each day. They usually sleep standing up. If they lie down, it is easier for a predator to attack.

Sometimes calves sleep lying down.

Giraffes have very good eyesight. Since they are so tall, they can spot a predator from far away.

When a herd drinks or sleeps, one giraffe keeps watch. It warns the others when danger is coming.

Giraffes look out for predators while a calf drinks from a watering hole.

Giraffes live about fifteen to twenty years in the wild. They may seem slow and quiet. But they are strong and powerful animals.

Giraffe Life Cycle

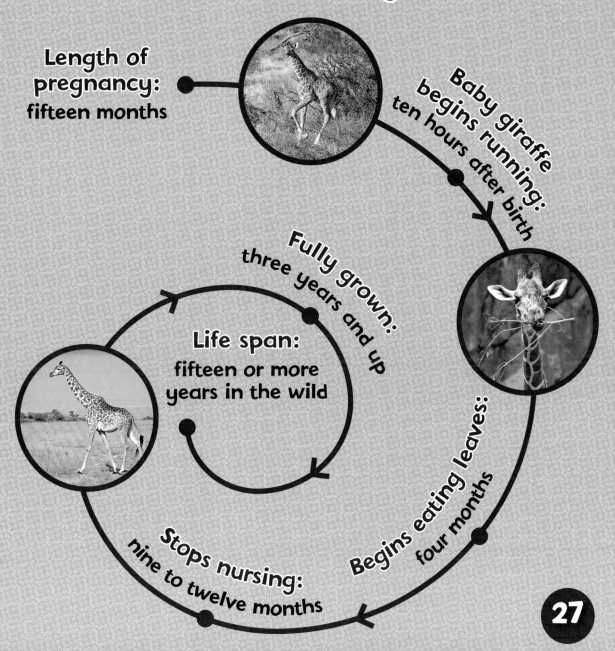

Length of pregnancy: fifteen months

Baby giraffe begins running: ten hours after birth

Fully grown: three years and up

Life span: fifteen or more years in the wild

Begins eating leaves: four months

Stops nursing: nine to twelve months

Habitat in Focus

- Giraffes live in dry savannas, grasslands, and open woodlands.

- Giraffes especially like leaves from acacia trees, which grow well in their habitat.

- In some areas, the giraffe's habitat is getting smaller. People use the land for farming and building. They cut down the acacia trees.

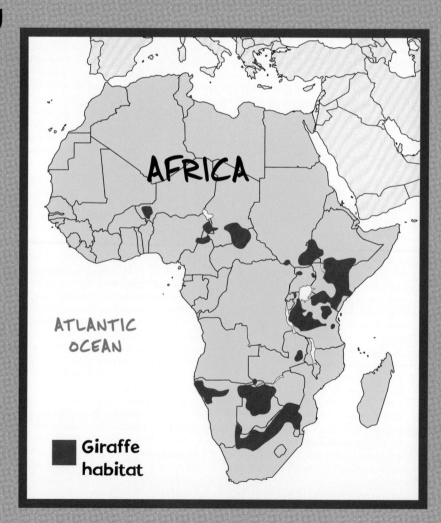

AFRICA

ATLANTIC OCEAN

Giraffe habitat

Fun Facts

- Giraffes are the tallest animals in the world.

- Giraffes have the same number of bones in their necks as humans do.

- Giraffe mothers stand up to give birth. The calf falls about 5 feet (1.5 m) to the ground.

- Giraffes can go many days without drinking. They get a lot of water from the trees they eat.

- Giraffes can run up to 35 miles (56 kilometers) per hour.

Glossary

bleat: the cry made by a giraffe

nurse: to drink milk from the mother

nursery group: a group of young giraffes watched over by an adult female

predator: an animal that hunts and kills other animals for food

water hole: a natural hole that contains water for drinking

Further Reading

Fort Wayne Children's Zoo:
Reticulated Giraffe
http://kidszoo.org/our-animals/african-journey
/reticulated-giraffe

Hughes, Catherine D. *Little Kids First Big Book of Animals.* Washington, DC: National Geographic, 2010.

National Geographic Kids: Giraffe
http://kids.nationalgeographic.com/content/kids
/en_US/animals/giraffe

San Diego Zoo Kids: Giraffe
http://kids.sandiegozoo.org/animals/mammals
/giraffe

Shea, Mary Molly. *Giraffes.* New York: Gareth Stevens Publishing, 2011.

Index

birth, 22

cud, 19

food, 16, 17, 18, 19, 23, 27

growth, 5, 15, 22, 27

herd, 8, 9, 10, 26
hooves, 12

life cycle, 27
life span, 27

mother giraffes, 4, 6, 7, 8, 12, 14, 16, 17, 18, 22

nursery group, 10
nursing, 16, 27

predators, 12, 24, 25

size, 5, 6
sleeping, 24, 26
sounds, 13

tongues, 17

water holes, 21

Photo Acknowledgments

The images in this book are used with the permission of: © Andrzej Kubik/Shutterstock Images, pp. 2, 22, 27 (bottom left); © Jonathan and Angela Scott/NHPA/Photoshot/Newscom, p. 4; © Phatthanit/Shutterstock Images, p. 5; © Ingram Publishing/Thinkstock, p. 6; © Jameson Weston/iStock/Thinkstock, p. 7; © Matt Ragen/Shutterstock Images, p. 8; © Oleg Znamenskiy/Shutterstock Images, p. 9; © MattiaATH/Shutterstock Images, p. 10; © Dennis W. Donohue/Shutterstock Images, pp. 11, 27 (top); © PicturesWild/Shutterstock Images, p. 12; © Molly Marshall/Shutterstock Images, p. 13; © Henk Bentlage/Shutterstock Images, p. 14; © Dan Kitwood/Getty Images News/Thinkstock, p. 15; © Marnie Mitchell-Lister/Shutterstock Images, pp. 16, 27 (bottom right); © James Ward Ewing/Shutterstock Images, p. 17; © Fuse/Thinkstock, p. 18; © nikom737/Shutterstock Images, p. 19; © Marc Turcan/Shutterstock Images, p. 20; © Humpata/iStock/Thinkstock, p. 21; © Piotr Gatlik/Shutterstock Images, p. 23; © Jandee Jones/iStock/Thinkstock, pp. 24, 31; © Joe McDonald/NHPA/Photoshot/Newscom, p. 25; © Stacey Ann Alberts/Shutterstock Images, p. 26; Red Line Editorial, 28; © GlobalP/iStock/Thinkstock, p. 30.

Front cover: © Andrew Yates/AFP/Getty Images.

Main body text set in Johann Light 30/36.